# Love to Dance

# Tap

Angela Royston

**Heinemann**
LIBRARY
Chicago, Illinois

Edited by Nancy Dickmann, Catherine Veitch, and Abby Colich
Designed by Cynthia Della-Rovere
Picture research by Elizabeth Alexander
Production by Alison Parsons
Originated by Capstone Global Library Ltd
Printed and bound in China by CTPS

16 15 14 13 12
10 9 8 7 6 5 4 3 2 1

**Library of Congress Cataloging-in-Publication Data**
Royston, Angela, 1945-
Tap / Angela Royston.—1st ed.
  p. cm.—(Love to dance)
Includes bibliographical references and index.
ISBN 978-1-4109-4923-3 (hb)—ISBN 978-1-4109-4928-8 (pb) 1. Tap dancing—Juvenile literature. I. Title.
GV1794.R69 2013
792.78—dc23                    2012019143

**Acknowledgments**
We would like to thank the following for permission to reproduce photographs: Alamy pp. 14 (© The Commercial Appeal/ZUMA Wire Service), 18 (© Photos 12), 24 (© Corbis Premium RF), 27 (© Neil Setchfield), 28 (© ZUMA Wire Service); Getty Images pp. 4 (Rob Elliott/AFP), 12 (John Kobal Foundation/Moviepix), 13 (Michael Ochs Archives), 15 (Mike Clarke/AFP), 17 (Ethan Miller), 19 (Chris Nash/Digital Vision), 20 (Donna Ward); Press Association p. 11 (AP Photo/Danny Johnston); Rex Features pp. 21 (c.Warner Br/Everett), 26 (Steven Peskett); Shutterstock title page (© AlenKadr), 6 (© Hasan Shaheed), 7 (© Hannamariah), 8 (© AlenKadr), 10 (© Sean Nel), 16 (© Sean Nel), 25 (© Sean Nel), 29 (© Losevsky Pavel); TopFoto pp. 5 (ArenaPAL/Clive Barda), 9 (PERSSON Johan/ArenaPAL), 22 (ArenaPAL/Francis Loney); Woolfson & Tay p. 23 (Shim Sham Tap Jam).

Design features reproduced with permission of Shutterstock (© Steve Wood, © L.Watcharapol).

Cover photograph of Tap Dogs performing at the Novello Theater, London, England, reproduced with permission Rex Features (Alastair Muir).

We would like to thank Annie Beserra for her invaluable help in the preparation of this book.

Every effort has been made to contact copyright holders of material reproduced in this book. Any omissions will be rectified in subsequent printings if notice is given to the publisher.

All the Internet addresses (URLs) given in this book were valid at the time of going to press. However, due to the dynamic nature of the Internet, some addresses may have changed, or sites may have changed or ceased to exist since publication. While the author and publisher regret any inconvenience this may cause readers, no responsibility for any such changes can be accepted by either the author or the publisher.

# Contents

Some words are shown in bold, **like this**. You can find out what they mean by looking in the glossary.

# This Is Tap Dancing!

Tap dancing is happy and exciting. It is amazing how fast tap dancers move their feet. The sound of tapping shoes is part of the music. Sometimes it is the only music!

## Why I dance

Champion tap dancer Justin Jackson says: "I'm really into tap dancing. The style that I do allows you to express yourself."

# How Tap Began

Tap became popular in the southern United States, when the dances and drum music of African Americans became mixed with Irish **step dances** and **clog** dances.

# Step dances

Jig shoes are not the best shoes for every dance! But theses jig shoes are perfect for **striking** the ground in Irish step dancing.

# What to Wear

Tap dancers wear special tap shoes. They have metal plates screwed to the **soles** of the toes and the heels. It is the metal plates that make the tapping sound when they hit the floor.

## Be comfortable

Some tap dancers dress up in fancy costumes when they perform on stage. But you can tap dance in any comfortable clothes.

# Basic Step: The Shuffle

The shuffle is a basic step. The dancer uses the **ball** of the foot to **brush** the floor going forward and then **strike** it on the way back.

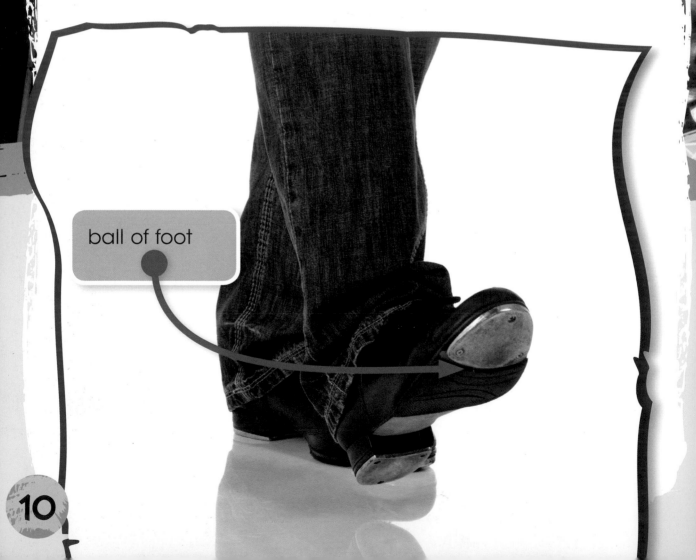

ball of foot

## The hop, shuffle, step

In the hop, shuffle, step, the dancer changes from one foot to the other with a hop and a shuffle in between.

# The Hollywood Years

In the 1930s actors often tap danced in movies. In *Singin' in the Rain*, Gene Kelly is so happy that he tap dances in heavy rain! Bill "Bojangles" Robinson was one of the first tap dance movie stars.

Fred Astaire and Ginger Rogers were famous for dance movies.

## Fast mover

Robinson claimed he could run backward faster than most people can run forward!

# Tap Dancing Skills

Tap dancers have good **rhythm**. They also need good balance and **coordination**—and lots of practice.

## Record-breaking skill

James Devine is the world's fastest tap dancer. He made 38 taps every second in a dance display in 1998!

# Tricky Move: Wings

In a wing, the dancer **brushes** one foot out to the side, **strikes** it on the way back, and then steps onto it. To make it harder, the dancer hops off the ground with the other foot!

brushing a foot

## Two feet together

The most spectacular way to do wings is to jump and do the move with both feet at the same time!

# Tap Dance Styles

There are different styles of tap dancing. In **rhythm** tap the dancers learn to **improvise**. This means they make up their own moves as they go along.

Gregory Hines was one of the most famous rhythm tap dancers.

## Flamenco

Flamenco is a dance from southern Spain. The dancers tap and stamp their feet and heels. Sometimes they click their fingers, too.

# A Living Legend

Savion Glover is the most amazing tap dancer today. His show *Bring in 'Da Noise, Bring in 'Da Funk* told the history of African Americans through tap dancing.

Glover amazed audiences in his show *Bare Soundz*.

## Happy Feet

*Happy Feet* is a cartoon movie about Mumble, a tap dancing penguin. Savion Glover provided the real dancing feet for the cartoon penguin.

# The Tap Dance Challenge

Sometimes dancers face off in a tap dance challenge. One tap dancer begins to dance while the other watches. They take turns trying to outdo each other's steps and **combinations**.

## The Shim Sham Shimmy

The Shim Sham Shimmy is a dance that all the dancers sometimes do together at the end of a performance or festival.

# Tricky Move: The Turn

More skilled tappers put several steps and turns together to make amazing **combinations**. One tricky move is to turn by crossing the feet and swiveling on the toes at the same time.

## Spotting

Spotting stops tap dancers from getting dizzy when they turn. Dancers start to turn their body whilst still facing the front. Then they whip their head around so their head and body is facing the front again.

# Where to See Tap

Tap dancing is popular today. You can see it in dance festivals, shows, and dancing competitions on television. You may even see someone tap dancing on the street.

Tap dancers perform on a reality competition television show.

These street dancers perform an *a cappella* tap dance.

# No music!

***A cappella*** tap dance is a tap dance with no music. The dancers have to keep perfect time by themselves. Some dancers also use their voice to imitate, or copy, the sounds of their feet.

# Give It a Try!

Tap dancing is fun to do and good exercise. You can stomp your feet and make a lot of noise! The best way to learn is to join a tap dance class.

## New steps

When you learn a new step,
do it slowly at first, and then
practice until you can do it fast.

# Glossary

**a cappella** without music. An *a cappella* tap dance is a tap dance with no music.

**ball** part of the sole of the foot between the toes and instep

**brush** in tap dancing, to brush is to bend the knee and strike the ball of the foot across the floor

**clog** strong, heavy shoe with a wooden sole

**combination** several steps joined together

**coordination** move different parts of the body at the same time

**improvise** make something up as you go along

**rhythm** regular pattern of sounds linked to the strong beat in a piece of music

**sole** part of your foot or shoe that touches the ground when you walk

**step dance** dance in which the movement of the feet is more important than moving the arms or other parts of the body—for example, an Irish step dance

**strike** hit

# Find Out More

## Books

Clay, Kathryn. *Tap Dancing*. Mankato, Minn.:
Capstone, 2010.

Feinstein, Stephen. *Savion Glover* (African-American
Heroes). Berkeley Heights, N.J.: Enslow, 2009.

Gamble, Nikki. *Tap and Jazz* (Dance).
Chicago: Heinemann Library, 2008.

Graves, Karen M. *Tap Dancing* (Snap Books).
Mankato, Minn.: Capstone, 2008.

## Websites

Facthound offers a safe, fun way to find Internet sites related
to this book. All of the sites on Facthound have been
researched by our staff.

Here's all you do:
Visit www.facthound.com

Type in this code: 9781410949233

# Index